Church Basics

Understanding Baptism

Series Editor Jonathan Leeman
Author Bobby Jamison

B&H
PUBLISHING GROUP
Nashville, Tennessee

978-1-4336-8887-4

Published by B&H Publishing Group
Nashville, Tennessee

Dewey Decimal Classification: 265.1
Subject Heading: BAPTISM \ CHURCH MEMBERSHIP \
SACRAMENTS

2 3 4 5 6 7 8 • 20 19 18 17 16

CONTENTS

CHURCH BASICS SERIES PREFACE

The Christian life is the churched life. This basic biblical conviction informs every book in the Church Basics series.

That conviction in turn affects how each author treats his topic. For instance, the Lord's Supper is not a private, mystical act between you and Jesus. It is a meal around the family table in which you commune with Christ and Christ's people. The Great Commission is not a license to head into the nations as Jesus' witness all by oneself. It is a charge given to the whole church to be fulfilled by the whole church. The authority of the church rests not only with the leaders, but with the entire assembly. Every member has a job to do, including you.

Every book is written *for* the average church member, and this is a crucial point. If the Christian life is a churched life, then you, a baptized believer and church member, have a responsibility to understand these basic topics. Just as Jesus charges you with promoting and protecting his gospel message, so he charges you with promoting and protecting his gospel people, the church. These books will explain how.

You are like a shareholder in Christ's gospel ministry corporation. And what do good shareholders do? They study their company, study the market, and study the competition. They want the most out of their investment. You, Christian, have invested your whole life in the gospel. The purpose of the series, then, is to help you maximize the health and kingdom profitability of your local congregation for God's glorious gospel ends.

Are you ready to get to work?

Jonathan Leeman
Series Editor

Books in the Church Basics series:

Introduction

Hello, and welcome to this brief book on baptism. I might even call it a "booklet." You can call it whatever you like. Would you like to come in and take a seat? I can show you around before we get started.

But first, let me tell you a little bit about you, or at least, who I expect you to be. If we were doing this in person, I'd ask you about yourself instead of telling you about yourself. But we're doing this in writing, so the best I can do is guess. My best guess is that there are basically three kinds of people who will read this book, all of them Christians.

If you're not a Christian, I'm glad this book found its way to you, but there are lots of other books about Christianity I'd encourage you to read first! Start with the four Gospels, and Greg Gilbert's book *Who Is Jesus?* (Crossway, 2015). And I'd encourage you to get together with a Christian friend to talk about the Bible and what it means to follow Jesus.

In any case, the first kind of person I expect to read this book is someone who believes in Jesus but hasn't yet been baptized. Maybe you don't really know what baptism is. Maybe you know what baptism is, but you aren't sure why you need to be baptized. Maybe you wonder if your "baptism" really was a baptism. You were an infant or were so young you don't know if your profession of faith was real. This book(let) will address all these questions. My goal for you is that, if you're a Christian who has not yet been baptized, this book will convince you to take the plunge. (Since it's impossible to write a book on baptism without at least one groan-inducing water pun, it's best to get it over with.)

A second group I hope will read this book are Christians who are simply interested in learning more about baptism. Surely there are at least a few of you out there. You've already been baptized, but you want to think more about this command that Jesus gave his church. Maybe you want to know better how to explain baptism to new believers or non-believers. I hope this book will provide biblical answers to questions you're asking—and even questions you're not asking but maybe should be.

A third kind of person I expect to read this book is a church leader, especially a pastor. By God's grace, pastors are often in the position to baptize new believers, and they also strongly influence how their church practices baptism and what their church recognizes as baptism. Pastors also set the pace for whether their church requires baptism for church membership, an increasingly debated issue.

I don't expect you will agree with every jot and tittle in this book. There are so many issues here that Christians disagree about. Nonetheless, I hope you will find it a useful resource for your members even in those places where you and I might disagree. And who knows, maybe I'll even persuade you! I have found it useful to give away books to church members even when I don't agree with everything in them—and I'll say so—just to get them thinking about the topic at hand.

Throughout the book I have all three audiences in mind. We begin with the question, "What is baptism?" in chapter 1. Chapter 2 asks, "Who should be baptized?" Chapter 3 biblically evaluates the practice of infant baptism. In chapter 4 I demonstrate why the Bible requires baptism—that is, believer's baptism—for church membership. Chapter 5 examines a few scenarios in which something Christians are calling "baptism" actually isn't. And chapter 6 offers some practical guidance for how churches should go about baptizing believers.

Before writing this little book, I wrote a heftier one called *Going Public: Why Baptism Is Required for Church Membership* (B&H Academic, 2015). That book aims more directly at church leaders and focuses tightly on the question implied in its subtitle. I borrow heavily from *Going Public* in chapter 4, moderately in chapter 6, and sparingly in a few other places. My thanks to the publisher for permitting this borrowing.

My thanks to you for taking the time to read this book. I pray it helps you follow Jesus and help others follow Jesus.

CHAPTER 1

What Is Baptism?

What would you do if you were wading in a swimming pool and a friend came up behind you and dunked you under the water? You could simply forgive your friend—a solidly Christian move. You could retaliate in kind. You could even escalate the aquatic conflict, waiting until your friend got out and dried off before shoving him or her back into the pool. So, which will it be?

Take two: what would you do if your friend sneaked up behind you, dunked you, and then said, "Now you've been baptized!" Even if you know little about baptism, my guess is you'll have a strong suspicion that, in addition to being slightly odd, your friend is wrong. You haven't been baptized; all you've been is dunked.

But what would it take to turn this dunking into baptism? It seems obvious that you'd have to lose the element of surprise and participate knowingly and willingly. But don't some churches baptize infants? Babies don't consent to be baptized. What about the one doing the dunking? Would your friend have to be a pastor? Would it have to take place in church rather than a swimming pool?

Baptism Is . . .

This chapter answers the question, "What is baptism?" I will first explain and defend a biblical understanding of baptism and then offer a few brief comments about what baptism isn't. If you've been holding off on baptism because you're not sure what it is, I hope this chapter will sweep away that confusion and clear your way to obeying Jesus' command to be baptized.

Here we go, then: *baptism is a church's act of affirming and portraying a believer's union with Christ by immersing him or her in water, and a believer's act of publicly committing him or herself to Christ and his people, thereby uniting a believer to the church and marking off him or her from the world.* Let's walk through this definition phrase by phrase and see how each part arises from Scripture.

A Church's Act

Baptism is a church's act.[1] Consider first that baptism is something someone does to someone else. You don't baptize yourself; there are always two parties involved. And both parties say something to each other and to the world.

People today tend to think that baptism is a symbol that people can simply choose to place upon themselves, like deciding to buy a shirt at the store and then wearing it in public. It doesn't so much matter who is doing the baptizing, like it doesn't matter much who the clerk at the checkout counter happens to be. Any Christian can baptize, anywhere, because the focus is not on the baptizer. It's on the baptizee. *You* must decide to get baptized, because *you* want to make a public statement: "I'm with Jesus." Think of Philip and the Ethiopian eunuch in Acts 8. The eunuch wants to get baptized. He asks Philip to baptize him, which he does. It's all pretty simple, right?

In fact, the New Testament presents a fuller picture, and what we find in a passage like Acts 8 is actually the exception to the rule, not the rule. You have to start not in Acts, but back in Matthew 16 and 18, where Jesus gives the keys of the kingdom first to the apostles, and then to local churches. The keys of the kingdom are for binding on earth what's bound in heaven, and loosing on earth what's loosed in heaven. This means that the apostles and gathered churches both have the authority to make public a declaration or verdict on Jesus' behalf. Think about what a judge does when he pounds his gavel. He doesn't write the law. He doesn't make the defendant innocent or guilty. Rather, he looks at the law. He looks at the evidence. And then he declares a public—and binding—verdict.

This judge-like authority to make official declarations on heaven's behalf is something Jesus gives to gathered churches, not to individual Christians. Listen to Matthew 18:20: "For where two or three are gathered together in My name, I am there among them." Jesus is not talking to small groups here, and his presence among them is not a mystical experience or atmospheric condition. Read the context carefully and you'll see that Jesus is saying that his heavenly authority belongs to gathered churches (see especially verses 18–19). A church is a regular gathering of at least two or three people who together testify to Christ's name. And Christ is present with such gatherings to authorize them to speak in his name.

We need all this to understand what's happening in Matthew 28's Great Commission. First, Jesus reminds us he's the one with all authority in heaven and earth (v. 18). Next, he authorizes his disciples to baptize and to make disciples in the name of the Father, himself, and the Spirit (v. 19). Then he tells them to teach everything he has commanded, which is fulfilled in the ongoing teaching ministry of the local church (v. 20a). Finally, he reaffirms that his authoritative presence is there in that church: "And remember, I am with you always, to the end of the age" (v. 20b). Matthew 28 very much has the stipulations and authorizations of Matthew 16 and 18 in the background. Jesus didn't forget what he said back there, and neither should we.

So the question is: who has the authority to baptize? Any Christian? Well, if you're on the missions frontier, where no other Christians exist, then you have no choice. Yes, you baptize. Since no local church yet exists, you *are* the church in that place. And Acts 8 provides a precedent for you if you are ever in this situation. At the same time, recall that Jesus explicitly ties his authoritative presence to churches—to two or three people (or two or three thousand) gathered in his name. Ordinarily, therefore, it is local churches who have the authority to baptize. Since baptism is performed by an individual, the church acts through a representative. But baptism is still a church's act.

This doesn't mean a church has the authority to deny baptism to someone who gives evidence of being converted (see Acts 11:17–18). But it does mean that, ordinarily, a church's consent should be involved because it's not just the baptizee who makes a public statement. The baptizer *also* makes a public statement or verdict. They "go on record" on earth for the kingdom of heaven, which brings us to the next point.

Of Affirming and Portraying a Believer's Union with Christ

What exactly does the church say in baptism? In baptism a church affirms a believer's profession of faith in Christ. It affirms that someone who claims to be united to Christ in his death and resurrection, so far as they can discern, is. It sets a visible, public seal to an invisible, spiritual reality.

Faith unites us to Christ so that we experience all the benefits of his death and resurrection. Baptism signifies this union. Consider the following passages:

> Or are you unaware that all of us who were baptized into Christ Jesus were baptized into His death? Therefore we were buried with Him by baptism into death, in order that, just as Christ was raised from the dead by the glory of the Father, so we too may walk in a new way of life. (Rom. 6:3–4)

> But since that faith has come, we are no longer under a guardian, for you are all sons of God through faith in Christ Jesus. For as many of you as have been baptized into Christ have put on Christ like a garment. (Gal. 3:25–27)

Baptism is a sign of the gospel's application. It is a sign that *this person* has turned from sin and has been united to Christ by faith. But baptism doesn't just affirm these realities; it also portrays them. Think of Christ dying, being buried, and rising again. Baptism publicly pictures someone's union with this death, burial, and resurrection. A person is physically plunged under water and raised out of it.

And because baptism pictures our union with Christ, it also pictures the benefits of that union. Through Christ our sins are forgiven and cleansed; baptism signifies both. Peter said to the crowd at Pentecost, "Repent . . . and be baptized, each of you, in the name of Jesus Christ for the forgiveness of your sins" (Acts 2:38). And Ananias told the newly converted apostle Paul, "And now, why delay? Get up and be baptized, and wash away your sins by calling on His name" (Acts 22:16). Further, through Christ we experience a new, Spirit-powered life, and baptism's symbolic resurrection signifies this life (Rom. 6:4; Col. 2:11–12). In baptism a church affirms that someone who professes faith in Christ is in fact united to Christ, and it dramatically depicts that union and all its benefits.

By Immersing Him or Her in Water

How does a church affirm and portray a believer's union with Christ? By immersing him or her in water. The Greek word *baptizō*, on which our word "baptize" is based, means to dip or plunge something in water, typically resulting in complete submersion. The New Testament consistently portrays baptism as immersion. John the Baptist baptized "in Aenon near Salim, because there was plenty of water there" (John 3:23), and there's no indication that the baptisms performed by Jesus' disciples required any less water.

Further, when the Ethiopian eunuch came to faith in Christ while riding in his chariot with Philip, he said, "Look, there's water! What would keep me from being baptized?" (Acts 8:36). And we read, "Then he ordered the chariot to stop, and both Philip and the eunuch went down into the water, and he baptized him. When they came up out of the water, the Spirit of the Lord carried Philip away, and the eunuch did not see him any longer. But he went on his way rejoicing"

(Acts 8:38–39). Baptism apparently required more water than they had in the chariot, so they went down into the water to perform it.

Finally, the apostle Paul's description of baptism as signifying a believer's death, burial, and resurrection with Christ seems to presuppose immersion (Rom. 6:1–4). Immersion physically mimics the motions of burial and resurrection, dramatizing our union with Christ in his. So a church affirms and portrays a believer's union with Christ by immersing him or her in water.

And a Believer's Act

But of course baptism isn't just a church's act—it is also a believer's act. A church baptizes; a Christian gets baptized. Consider how those who heard Peter preach at Pentecost responded to his message:

> When they heard this, they came under deep conviction and said to Peter and the rest of the apostles: "Brothers, what must we do?"
>
> "Repent," Peter said to them, "and be baptized, each of you, in the name of Jesus Christ for the forgiveness of your sins, and you will receive the gift of the Holy Spirit. For the promise is for you and for your children, and for all who are far off, as many as the Lord our God will call." . . . So those who accepted his message were baptized, and that day about 3,000 people were added to them. (Acts 2:37–39, 41)

Those who repented of sin and trusted in Jesus were baptized. Baptism is the first public act of the faith that receives Christ as Savior and Lord. If you're a Christian, Jesus commands you to be baptized. It's something you must do; no one else can do it for you.

And of course baptism isn't something non-Christians should do. Baptism affirms and portrays a believer's union with Christ, so only those united to Christ by faith should do it.

Of Publicly Committing Him or Herself to Christ

What is a believer doing in baptism? Publicly committing him or herself to Christ. Baptism is how you go on record as a Christian. It's how you publicly profess your faith in and submission to the Lord Jesus Christ.

In order to respond to the gospel, we are commanded to turn to Jesus both inwardly and outwardly, and the outward declares the inward. Baptism is performed in the open, before witnesses. Think about those who repented and were baptized at Pentecost. All those who stepped forward from the crowd to be baptized were marking themselves as Jesus' followers.

And that's exactly what Jesus wants—followers everyone can see. "Therefore, everyone who will acknowledge Me before men, I will also acknowledge him before My Father in heaven. But whoever denies Me before men, I will also deny him before My Father in heaven" (Matt. 10:32–33). There are no secret disciples of Jesus. The only way to follow Jesus is to do so openly, in plain sight, where everyone can see you. And baptism is how we declare ourselves, before the church and the world, to belong to Jesus. Jesus wants a spotlight trained on his disciples so that the world sees him reflected in us. Baptism is how we step into that light.

If you're uneasy about going public with your faith, look at baptism as a help rather than a hurdle. Jesus hasn't left it up to your boldness or creativity to figure out how to declare yourself a Christian; he's shown you how to do it. He's made it simple. All you have to do is profess your faith in Christ and then lean back and hold your breath.

But baptism is not just the profession of a prior commitment; it is itself the making of a commitment. Peter writes of how Noah and his family were saved through the waters of judgment, and then draws a comparison: "Baptism, which corresponds to this, now saves you (not the removal of the filth of the flesh, but the pledge of a good conscience toward God) through the resurrection of Jesus Christ" (1 Pet. 3:21). When Peter says that baptism "saves you," he clarifies that what saves is not physical washing with water but the faith that baptism expresses. And Christ's resurrection is what powers faith. It's not that there is any power or virtue in our faith itself. Instead, by faith we take hold of the resurrected Christ.

The phrase "pledge of a good conscience" could be taken as a petition, a promise, or both. I think both are present in baptism, even if this verse highlights one or the other. Baptism is a petition, a prayer that gives voice to faith's plea: "Save me, Lord Jesus!" By identifying with Christ's death and resurrection in baptism, a believer publicly claims Christ as his or her Savior, asking God to make good on his promise to save.

Baptism is a promise in that it publicly pledges submission to Christ as Lord. To be baptized into Christ's name (Matt. 28:19) is to submit to his authority. Baptism is an oath of allegiance to King Jesus. It is how you publicly swear fidelity to him. In that sense baptism is a promise to obey all that Christ commands. To be baptized is to sign on the dotted line below "Observe Everything I Have Commanded You" (Matt. 28:20). You can't receive Jesus as Savior without revering him as Lord. In baptism we take up the easy yoke that is also a cross, walking in all the ways of Jesus.

Baptism is where faith goes public. It is where we put on Jesus' team jersey. Baptism is how a believer commits him or herself to Christ—owning him as Savior and submitting to him as Lord—in plain view of all.

And His People

In baptism a believer commits him or herself not just to Christ but also to Christ's people. Recall again what happened at Pentecost: "So those who accepted his message were baptized, and that day about 3,000 people were added to them" (Acts 2:41). To whom were these 3,000 added? To the church in Jerusalem, which previously numbered only 120 (Acts 1:15). Those who were baptized at Pentecost stepped out of the world and into the church. And so it is—or so it should be—with everyone who is baptized today.

To trust in Jesus is to join the company of all who trust in Jesus. To receive Jesus is to receive his people. The gospel not only reconciles us to God (Eph. 2:1–10), it also reconciles us to each other (Eph. 2:11–22). To call on God as Father is to embrace all others who do the same as brothers and sisters. To be united to Christ is to become a member of his body (1 Cor. 12:12–26; Eph. 1:23; Col. 1:18; 1 Pet. 2:10).

So in baptism, a believer commits him or herself to both Christ and his people. In putting on the team jersey you commit to playing on the team. In baptism you step out of the world into the church. There's no in-between zone where you're out there with Jesus but not yet with his people. To join yourself to Jesus is to join his people. Baptism, then, is a commitment to follow Christ in the company of his church. In baptism a Christian commits to loving, serving, and submitting to Christ's people.

Thereby Uniting a Believer to the Church and Marking Off Him or Her from the World

In transacting this commitment, the church makes a commitment of its own. The act of baptism conveys the believer's commitment, "I hereby pledge myself to Christ and to you, his people," and it conveys the church's commitment, "We hereby affirm your profession and pledge ourselves to you, a member of Christ's body." In baptism the believer speaks to God and the church, and the church speaks for God to the individual.

So, when a church affirms and portrays a believer's union with Christ, and a believer commits himself to Christ and his people, that believer is united to the church and marked off from the world. The believer is added to the team roster and given its jersey to wear. Baptism publicly identifies someone as a Christian. In baptism, the church says to the world, "Look here! This one belongs to Jesus!" And because baptism identifies someone as a Christian, it initiates that person into the company of the church, Christ's new covenant people on earth.

We'll think more about baptism's uniting-to-the-church and marking-off-from-the-world function in chapter 4. For now, it's enough to see that in baptism a believer commits him or herself not only to Christ but also to his people.

Baptism Isn't . . .

Let's consider two brief comments on what baptism isn't. First, baptism itself does not save you. Remember that in 1 Peter 3:21, when Peter says that baptism saves, it's *not* that the physical washing has intrinsic power, but that baptism expresses faith in Christ's powerful resurrection. We are saved through trusting in Jesus' death and resurrection, and baptism is where that trust goes public.

Scripture is clear that *through faith* our sins are forgiven, we're counted righteous by God, and we're reconciled to God (Rom. 3:21–31; 4:1–8; 5:1–11). Baptism depicts all these realities, but it doesn't create them. All believers are commanded to be baptized, and obeying Christ's commands is how we demonstrate that our faith is real (John 14:21–24; James 2:14–26; 1 John 2:3–6). So no Christian should opt out of baptism on the grounds that it isn't "necessary for salvation." If you claim to be saved, baptism is necessary proof. Yet baptism itself doesn't guarantee salvation. The thief on the cross went to heaven without it (Luke 23:39–43), and Simon the magician was headed to hell with it (Acts 8:13–24).

Second, it's important to recognize that baptism isn't a mere human tradition. It's not something the church invented. It's not something we Christians only happen to do and could just as well not do. Instead, it's a command from Christ that is binding on all believers in all places at all times.

Next Up

Let's return to your dunking friend. If he succeeds in immersing you in the chlorinated, 78-degree water, has he baptized you?

Nope. But if you only had a hunch about this at the beginning of the chapter, hopefully now you have a clear biblical picture of what baptism is. In baptism, Jesus has given his disciples a way to openly own him as theirs and declare themselves his. And he's given the church a powerful and public way to both affirm and picture a believer's union with Christ. And in this twofold act, the believer commits to the church and the church commits to the believer. Baptism is a sign that both portrays a believer's union with Christ and effects a new, horizontal union, joining together the believer and the church.

What is baptism? Say it with me: *baptism is a church's act of affirming and portraying a believer's union with Christ by immersing him or her in water, and a believer's act of publicly committing him or herself to Christ and his people, thereby uniting a believer to the church and marking off him or her from the world.* That leads to our next question, and chapter: Who should be baptized?

CHAPTER 2

Who Should Be Baptized?

Do you consider yourself a Christian? If not, I'm glad you're reading this book, but baptism isn't your first priority. What you need to do first is turn from your sin and trust in Christ to save you.

But I assume that if you're reading this book, most likely you profess faith in Christ. If so, have you been baptized? Why or why not?

This chapter asks the question, "Who should be baptized?" And the answer is, "Every Christian." No exceptions, no special cases, no ifs, ands, or buts. In this chapter I'll set out the biblical mandate for baptism, explore some benefits of baptism, and answer objections to being baptized. One of these objections—that someone was already "baptized" as an infant—deserves special treatment, so it gets its own chapter.

The Mandate of Baptism

As we saw in the last chapter, Jesus commands his disciples to make disciples: "All authority has been given to Me in heaven and on earth. Go, therefore, and make disciples of all nations, baptizing them in the name of the Father and of the Son and of the Holy Spirit, teaching them to observe everything I have commanded you" (Matt. 28:18–20). How do Jesus' disciples make disciples? By, first, preaching the gospel of the kingdom to them, just as Jesus did (Matt. 4:17, 23) and just as he had previously sent his disciples out to do (Matt. 10:5–7). So it's fair to say that the command "make disciples" implies preaching the gospel. You become a disciple of Jesus through embracing the message about Jesus.

But Jesus specifies two more steps in this process, two means by which the disciple-making mandate is to be carried out: Jesus' disciples are to baptize these new disciples and teach them to obey all of Jesus' commands.

Step 1: Preach the gospel.
Step 2: When people respond in faith, baptize them.
Step 3: Teach them to do everything Jesus commanded.

All those who become disciples are baptized. There's no category of unbaptized disciple.

Baptism is something a disciple must do, offering him or herself up to its symbolic death and resurrection. So it seems clear from the order of Jesus' statement that baptism is actually the first item on the list marked "Everything I Have Commanded You." After repenting and believing, baptism is the first command Jesus' followers are called to obey. As a brand-new follower of Jesus, baptism is the first thing you do.

It's no surprise, then, that in the same breath Peter tells his hearers at Pentecost to repent and be baptized: "Repent . . . and be baptized, each of you, in the name of Jesus Christ for the forgiveness of your sins, and you will receive the gift of the Holy Spirit" (Acts 2:38). And we've seen that many of them did so: "So those who accepted his message were baptized, and that day about 3,000 people were added to them" (Acts 2:41). Again, embracing the gospel and getting baptized go hand in hand. If you come to trust in Jesus, the first thing you need to do is publicly say so in baptism.

This also explains why, throughout the New Testament epistles, the writers assume that all their Christian readers are baptized. Paul argues that we who died to sin can no longer live in it, then asks, "Or are you unaware that all of us who were baptized into Christ Jesus were baptized into His death?" (Rom. 6:3). And Paul assures the Galatians that they are all sons of God through faith in Christ, and then explains, "For as many of you as have been baptized into Christ have put on Christ" (Gal. 3:27; cf. 1 Cor. 1:13; Col. 2:12). The arguments only work if all the readers had been baptized.

If you are a Christian and you have not been baptized, you need to be. It is not merely optional or recommended or wise or the best thing to do. It's required. And while being a disciple of Jesus means more than obeying Jesus' commands, it never means less. Our obedience to Jesus is the litmus test of our love for him. Those who trust in Jesus do what he says, and he tells those who trust in him to be baptized.

Two Benefits of Baptism

If you claim to believe in Jesus but have not been baptized, this should be enough. Jesus commands baptism, so you go do it. But if you're still hesitant, I want to spur you to obeying Jesus' command to be baptized by highlighting two benefits of baptism.

The first is that confessing faith strengthens faith. Baptism is an open declaration that you belong to Jesus. And if you're reluctant to openly declare yourself a follower of Jesus, then baptism is what you most need to do! Faith in Jesus is meant to redefine you: what's true about your past, present, and future, who your family is, and who has your highest allegiance. Baptism is a way of picturing and proclaiming all of these realities.

If you try to keep your faith private, it will wither and die. Like our bodies, faith is strengthened by exercise, and baptism is an exercise of faith. Baptism is faith-fueled action, and it's an action that sets the trajectory for our whole life of faith. To be a Christian is to be open about it. The Christian life is lived on stage, amidst the company of the church, before the watching world. And baptism is how we step into the spotlight.

The second related benefit is that baptism presents a ready-made opportunity for evangelism. Many family and friends who otherwise wouldn't come to church would gladly attend a baptism. If your guests don't know what baptism means, use the gospel to explain it; if they don't understand the gospel, use baptism to illustrate it. Just as you are plunged under the water and rise up again, so Jesus was plunged into death but emerged from it victorious. And all those who are united to Christ share in his victory, because through his death and resurrection our sins are forgiven and we're reconciled to God.

Objections to Getting Baptized

If you're a professing Christian but you haven't been baptized, why not? Let's consider a few possible objections to getting baptized.

Why do I need to make such a big, public fuss about being a Christian? Isn't faith something personal and private? Isn't it enough that I trust in Jesus? God knows my heart. We have already seen that Jesus will have no private followers, no secret disciples: "Therefore, everyone who will acknowledge Me before men, I will also acknowledge him before My Father in heaven. But whoever denies Me before men, I will also deny him before My Father in heaven" (Matt. 10:32–33). And again, "For whoever is ashamed of Me and My words, the Son of Man will be ashamed of him when He comes in His glory and that of the Father and the holy angels" (Luke 9:26). Christians are those who confess faith in Christ. By definition, confession is a public act, speaking in someone's hearing. If you are nervous about going public as a Christian, view baptism as an aid rather than an obstacle. Being baptized helps you do with your faith what you need to do with it: share it openly.

A word to church leaders: I think it's generally a healthy practice to ask those being baptized not only to verbally confess faith in Christ and pledge obedience to him, but also to share how they personally came to trust in Jesus as Savior. This gives glory to God for his work in their life and heightens baptism's evangelistic power. But if someone has a paralyzing fear of public speaking, or is otherwise unable to narrate his or her testimony, I would encourage you to simply have the person assent to a confession of faith and commitment to obey Jesus. Something like this:

"Do you confess faith in Jesus Christ as your Savior and submit to him as Lord?"

"I do."

"Do you promise, depending on his grace, to obey Jesus in the fellowship of his church as long as you live?"

"I do."

I've been a believer for decades now. I wasn't baptized then, so why do I need to be baptized now after all this time? Since it's so long after my conversion, wouldn't it be meaningless anyway? Well, it certainly would have been better to get baptized as soon as you came to faith in Christ. But when it comes to obeying Christ's commands, late is definitely better than never (Matt. 21:28–32). And the time that has passed doesn't make the command any less binding. Sure, getting baptized now will mean admitting that you were wrong not to get baptized for all these years. But that's simply what it means to follow Jesus. When we discover sin in our lives, we repent and obey. "I have not come to call the righteous, but sinners to repentance" (Luke 5:32).

I don't know where to go to get baptized. Well, that presents a problem! Here's my advice: find a church that preaches the gospel and teaches the Bible. Find a church where people are serious about following Jesus and helping others follow Jesus. Introduce yourself to that church's leaders. Let them know you're a believer in Jesus and you want to be baptized. And commit to joining that church, serving in the church, and letting the church help you grow more like Christ. If you need help finding churches like this, the 9Marks church search should be a good place to start.[2]

I was already baptized as an infant. Baptism is a one-time gig. Once you've been baptized you don't need to, and shouldn't, be baptized again. But should infants be baptized? Is infant baptism really baptism? That's the subject of our next chapter.

The Bottom Line

If you've been delaying baptism out of anxiety or fear, take heart. Jesus promises that when we're hauled into court for his sake, his own Spirit will speak through us, giving us the words we need to say (Matt. 10:19–20). How much more will the Spirit who grants faith enable you to publicly confess that faith (1 Cor. 12:3)?

The bottom line is, every Christian is commanded to be baptized. So what are you waiting for?

CHAPTER 3

What about Infant Baptism?

What about infant baptism? I'm sure some people reading this were baptized as infants and now have serious doubts about whether that really was baptism. Or maybe you know that some churches practice infant baptism, but you have never considered why or evaluated the practice in light of Scripture.

In this chapter we'll lay out the most compelling theological rationale for infant baptism, assess it biblically, and then answer paedobaptist objections to the believer's baptism position.

The Case for Infant Baptism

For most of church history, at least a portion of churches have "baptized" infants, a position known as paedobaptism. Churches have done this for different reasons. Roman Catholics and some others believe that baptism actually imparts saving grace to the recipient and joins him or her to Christ's spiritual body. The act works of itself, so the infant recipient need not exercise faith or express consent in order for baptism to do its job. But this understanding of baptism is at odds with the gospel itself. Being joined to Christ by faith is what saves us. The ordinances of baptism and the Lord's Supper portray and ratify that union; they do not effect it.

Some Lutherans, following Luther himself, hold that infants who are baptized actually have faith. But then why do such huge numbers of those who are baptized as infants never show any evidence of faith? Where did their faith go?

Among evangelicals, Christians in the Reformed tradition offer the strongest argument for baptizing infants, which focuses on the relationship between God's covenants and their covenant signs.[3] A covenant is a relationship God freely enters with people which he ratifies by an oath. Covenants often come with signs that vividly portray something of the terms and benefits of the covenant. God's covenant with Abraham came with the covenant sign of circumcision, which continued under the Mosaic covenant (Gen. 17:1–14; Lev. 12:3). God made a covenant with Abraham and instructed him to circumcise all his male offspring. God's covenant included Abraham's offspring, as did the covenant sign.

Reformed Christians highlight continuities throughout the historical unfolding of God's plan of salvation. They affirm, rightly, that God has one plan of salvation he enacts through time, and that all those who experience this salvation belong to his one true people. They also argue that there is one "covenant of grace" in which all believers throughout history participate. This covenant finds its first expression in God's promise to Adam and Eve in the garden of Eden (Gen. 3:15), and it comes to fulfillment in Christ. And they generally argue that each of God's covenants with his people is an expression, or administration, of this one covenant of grace.

So, Reformed paedobaptists see a text like Acts 2:38–39 as expressing a principle common to both the Abrahamic covenant and the new covenant. After exhorting his hearers to repent and be baptized, Peter says, "For the promise is for you and for your children, and for all who are far off, as many as the Lord our God will call" (v. 39). Reformed paedobaptists argue that just as God extended his covenant promise with Abraham (and therefore the covenant sign) to his people and their infant children, so also he extends his new covenant promise (and therefore the new covenant sign of baptism) to both believers and their children. B. B. Warfield summarized the case for infant baptism like this: "God established His Church in the days of Abraham and put children into it. They must remain there until He puts them out. He has nowhere put them out. They are still then members of His Church and as such entitled to its ordinances."[4]

The Case against Infant Baptism

I have great respect and affection for paedobaptist Christians who argue along these lines. Some of them are my close friends or historical heroes. And the arguments I've sketched above display careful attention to Scripture and reverence for Scripture. Yet I don't think they're persuasive. Here are six reasons why.

1. Paedobaptism applies the sign of union with Christ to those who are not united to Christ. It divorces the sign from the reality.

Baptism is a sign of a believer's union with Christ in his death, burial, and resurrection (Rom. 6:1–4; Col. 2:11–12). But infants are not united to Christ. All people, even those born of Christian parents, must receive Christ by faith in order to be joined to him by the Spirit.

Some children who grow up in Christian homes don't remember a time when they didn't believe in Jesus, but that doesn't mean they were born believing in Jesus. The Spirit had to grant them faith and bring about repentance. They had to be transferred from the dominion of Satan into the dominion of the Son (Col. 1:13). They had to be raised from death to life, rescued from the prince of this world, saved from God's wrath (Eph. 2:1–3).

But paedobaptism applies the sign of union with Christ to those who are not united to Christ. It divorces the sign from the reality it expresses. In doing this, paedobaptism turns baptism into a contradiction. Baptism is a sign that the gospel has taken effect in someone's life, bringing forgiveness, cleansing, reconciliation, rebirth, new life. But paedobaptism extends the sign where none of these realities are present. Infant children of believers are not united to Christ by faith, so churches should not baptize them.

2. Paedobaptism confuses being born of Christian parents with being born again by the Spirit.

Another way to say this is that paedobaptism confuses being born of Christian parents with being born again by the Spirit. I'm not saying that all paedobaptist Christians confuse these two things in their minds; I'm saying their *practice* confuses them. A paedobaptist Christian may well know that his infant son needs to come to faith in Christ in order to be born again by the Spirit, but in having him baptized, the act itself attests that he already is.

The Westminster Confession says that the efficacy of the baptism is not tied to the time of its administration. In other words, an infant baptism is still valid even if the recipient comes to faith in Christ years afterward. But the problem is, the sign itself speaks. The sign itself says, "This one is united to Christ. This one has been buried and raised with Christ. This one has passed from death to new life in Christ." If paedobaptists want a sign that signifies the future possibility of union with Christ, they'll have to find something other than baptism. Baptism speaks in the present tense.

As a result, paedobaptism effectively communicates that the new birth is something you inherit by natural birth. It signifies that the infant children of believers are in a fundamentally different spiritual condition than other infant children. Certainly believers' children are in a different spiritual environment than those of unbelievers—see below. But infant baptism says there's not just a difference in their environment but *in them*. Whatever welcome theological distinctions paedobaptists make, their practice confuses being born of Christian parents with being born again by the Spirit.

3. Paedobaptism mistakenly assumes that God is forming his new covenant people the same way he formed his old covenant people.

Further, paedobaptism mistakenly assumes that, in at least one crucial way, God is forming his new covenant people the same way he formed his old covenant people. Under the old covenant, God formed his people by familial descent into a distinct ethnic group. Under the new covenant, God forms his people by his Word and Spirit into a people gathered from all nations who call on his name.

Remember that the paedobaptist argument rests on a strong analogy between baptism and circumcision. God commanded Abraham to circumcise his offspring, in part, so that the descendants of Abraham would be an identifiable ethnic people, distinct from the world around them. This purpose of creating a nation came to fruition with the Exodus and the giving of the Mosaic covenant at Sinai—what Scripture elsewhere calls "the old covenant" (2 Cor. 3:14). When God called Israel out of Egypt, he brought them to himself and gave them a special role. They were to obey his law in order to be his treasured possession among all peoples, and to serve as a kingdom of priests and a holy nation (Exod. 19:4–6).

God set Israel on the world stage to show the nations what he is like. He wanted Israel to walk in his ways so that all the surrounding nations would sit up and take note (Deut. 4:1–8). And he distinguished Israel from those nations, first and foremost, by circumcision. All male children in Israel had to be circumcised (Gen. 17:12), and all foreigners who wanted to join the people of Israel had to be circumcised (Exod. 12:48). From the call of Abraham to the coming of Christ, God's people were marked off from the world by circumcision.

Throughout that time, a circumcised male Israelite was a member of God's people whether or not his spiritual state matched his circumcised status. Circumcision signified consecration to God, and it demanded that those set apart to God live lives set apart to God. That's why God commanded his people, "Therefore, circumcise your hearts and don't be stiff-necked any longer" (Deut. 10:16; cf. Jer. 4:4). But of course, not everyone who was circumcised in flesh was circumcised in heart. In fact, as the whole story of Israel shows, most of God's people under the old covenant disobeyed him. They worshiped idols and committed injustice and immorality. Their kings, princes, prophets, priests, and the people as a whole turned from the Lord and provoked him to anger (Jer. 32:30–33). The wickedness of the people grew so great that God eventually expelled his people from their land, calling down the curses of the covenant on them: first Israel in the north, then Judah in the south (Deut. 28:15–68; 2 Kings 17:6–23; 25:1–21).

So God had a plan for Israel, a plan to manifest his glory to all nations through them. He gave them the old covenant so that they would obey and flourish and be distinct from the nations, testifying to his incomparable wisdom. But the people's hearts were corrupt. Their sin ran deeper than any solution the law could bring. They had every advantage—the law, worship in the temple, God's glory dwelling in their midst (Rom. 9:4)—and yet all those advantages proved no advantage in the end. Too many of those in the covenant failed to keep the covenant. They disobeyed and were judged.

What God's people needed was a heart transplant. And that's exactly what God promised to give them in the new covenant.

> "Look, the days are coming"—this is the Lord's declaration—
> "when I will make a new covenant with the house of Israel and
> with the house of Judah. This one will not be like the covenant
> I made with their ancestors when I took them by the hand to
> bring them out of the land of Egypt—a covenant they broke
> even though I had married them"—the Lord's declaration.
> "Instead, this is the covenant I will make with the house of
> Israel after those days"—the Lord's declaration. "I will put My
> teaching within them and write it on their hearts. I will be their
> God, and they will be My people. No longer will one teach his
> neighbor or his brother, saying, 'Know the Lord,' for they will

all know Me, from the least to the greatest of them"—this is the
LORD's declaration. "For I will forgive their wrongdoing and
never again remember their sin." (Jer. 31:31–34)

The Lord emphatically declares that this covenant will not be like
the covenant he made with Israel on Mount Sinai after bringing them
out of Egypt. How will it differ? They won't break this one (v. 32).

Why won't they break this covenant? Because God will put his
teaching, his *torah*, within them and will write it on their hearts (v. 33).
God's law won't be something outside the people, standing over against
them as a bare demand. Instead, it will live within them, welling up
from inside, directing them to walk in God's ways.

One chapter later the Lord makes the same promise in other
words when he says, "I will give them one heart and one way so that
for their good and for the good of their descendants after them, they
will fear Me always. I will make an everlasting covenant with them: I
will never turn away from doing good to them, and I will put fear of
Me in their hearts so they will never again turn away from Me" (Jer.
32:39–40). This new covenant will be everlasting because God himself
will enable his people to fear him so that they obey him, cling to him,
and never again turn away from him. This is another way of saying
that he will circumcise the people's hearts, doing for them what they
could never do for themselves (Deut. 30:6).

God makes the same promise in yet another way when he declares
in Ezekiel, "I will give you a new heart and put a new spirit within you;
I will remove your heart of stone and give you a heart of flesh. I will
place My Spirit within you and cause you to follow My statutes and
carefully observe My ordinances" (Ezek. 36:26–27). God will give his
people new hearts and will even cause his Spirit to dwell within them,
with the result that they obey his will in a way they never have before.
Law on their heart, one heart and one way, circumcised hearts, a heart
of flesh and not stone, God's Spirit within—all these are ways of saying

that in the new covenant, God's people will know God and obey God because God himself will transform them from the inside out.

Notice also that in the new covenant promise of Jeremiah 31, neighbors won't have to say "Know the LORD" to each other, "for they will all know Me, from the least to the greatest of them" (v. 34). All of God's people will know God. What is implicit in all the promises we've just considered God here makes explicit; all his people will be transformed. All those in the covenant will fulfill the covenant. All those marked off as God's people will truly live as God's people. This new covenant will finally close the gap between covenant belonging and covenant keeping. That is its very reason for existence.

The people spurned the covenant God made with them at Sinai, and they suffered the devastation of exile as the just reward for their sin. But in the new covenant, all God's people—not just some—will know and serve God. All God's people will have their sins forgiven (v. 34). All God's people will truly be God's people, not just outwardly but inwardly. This is precisely what makes the new covenant new, what makes it decisively different from how God related to his people through the Mosaic covenant (v. 31).

In Christ's death and resurrection, God has now inaugurated this new covenant (Luke 22:20; Heb. 9:15). And at Pentecost, God poured out his Spirit on his people as he promised in the prophets (Acts 2:1–41). Ever since, he has been calling his new covenant people to himself by his Word and Spirit.

In the old covenant, God formed his people by marking off the descendants of Abraham as a distinct ethnicity. He gave them circumcision, and his whole law, so that they would be distinct from the world. But not all who were circumcised in flesh were circumcised in heart. Not all who were in the covenant kept the covenant. God's people were identifiable by circumcision regardless of their spiritual state.

But in the new covenant, God is forming his people in a radically different way. God is no longer propagating an ethnic community by familial descent. Instead, by his Spirit applying the word of the gospel to people's hearts, God is calling the people of the new covenant out of every nation. God is forming his new covenant people by giving them new birth. The way into God's new covenant people—the only way—is to be born again by the Spirit.

Paedobaptism mistakenly assumes that, in a crucial way, God is forming his new covenant people the same way he formed his old covenant people, by familial descent. Paedobaptists extend the covenant sign of baptism to infant children of believers because they believe those infants are included in the new covenant. But a person enters the new covenant not by natural birth, but by spiritual rebirth. All those in the new covenant have their sins forgiven and know the Lord. All those in the new covenant have God's law written on their hearts. All those in the new covenant have God's Spirit living in them, renewing them, enabling them to walk in God's ways. Being born to Christian parents is no guarantee that these new covenant realities will be true for someone.

The new covenant does not operate by birth but by rebirth. So the sign of the new covenant should only be given to those who give evidence of that rebirth by their profession of faith in Christ.

4. Paedobaptism undermines the church's saltiness and lightness (Matt. 5:13–16).

God's old covenant people were, by design, a spiritually mixed bag. The physical sign of circumcision came before, and with no guarantee of, the spiritual reality of a circumcised heart. But this is precisely what God changes in the new covenant. By design, the new covenant people are all renewed, all forgiven, all indwelt by the Spirit.

Yes, some non-Christians do inevitably join the church. But that's not by design! That's like saying that some married people lust and commit adultery. Yes, they do, but they shouldn't! This is precisely why Jesus instituted church discipline (Matt. 18:15–20). Those whose unrepentant lives demonstrate that they are not members of the new covenant are to be excluded from the new covenant community. The very fact that Jesus commands this indicates that the church, unlike Israel under the old covenant, is intended to be a community of those who all know the Lord.

Paedobaptism brings into the new covenant community on earth those who do not participate in the realities of the new covenant. It puts people in the church before they're in Christ. It makes church members of those who are not Christians. Inevitably, this will weaken the church's witness to Christ. It's a lot more traumatic to excommunicate a nineteen-year-old who was baptized as an infant and is now sinning unrepentantly than it is to simply wait to baptize a young person until they credibly profess faith in Christ.

So, despite the noble intentions of Christians who practice paedobaptism, baptizing infants will make the church's salt less salty, its light less bright (Matt. 5:13–16). Paedobaptism will, over time, make the church more like the world, because it brings the world into the church.

5. Paedobaptism dissolves two crucial differences between baptism and circumcision.

Paedobaptism also dissolves two crucial differences between baptism and circumcision. First, part of circumcision's role was to mark off God's people as a distinct ethnic entity. Circumcision accomplished this purpose whether or not the person circumcised was circumcised in heart. Circumcision was part of the means by which God formed his old covenant people along ethnic, familial lines. Sometimes proponents of paedobaptism tend to highlight circumcision's spiritual aspect to the point where they entirely overlook its ethnic, political function. Baptism, by contrast, pictures another line of descent entirely: being born again by the spirit.

Second, circumcision marked an Israelite as belonging to God. It consecrated a person to God, ushering him in to God's "holy"—that is, set apart—nation. As such, circumcision pointed toward the need for God's people to consecrate their hearts and lives to God in order to align with their covenantal status. God's people Israel were already circumcised, but the Lord charged them to circumcise themselves inwardly, to circumcise their hearts (Deut. 10:16; Jer. 4:4). And the very act of cutting off a part of a man's body threatened the fate that the man himself would suffer—being cut off from God's presence and people—if he disobeyed the covenant (Gen. 17:11–14). In other words, circumcision bore a demand for holiness. It pointed to the Israelites' need for a new nature.

Baptism, on the other hand, testifies that a person has been born again, has received a new self, has been inwardly renewed by the Spirit. Baptism testifies that a person *is* united to Christ and has new life in him. The New Testament doesn't tell believers, "Therefore, baptize your hearts and don't be stiff-necked any longer" (cf. Deut. 10:16). Instead, it tells believers, "Remember that you have been baptized. Don't keep living in sin; you've already died to it! Live out the new, resurrection life that's yours in Christ" (cf. Rom. 6:1–4). Baptism points to the promise of new life fulfilled in Christ in the life of a believer. Circumcision consecrated a person in status and demanded consecration of the heart; baptism says that heart consecration has happened in Christ.

Paedobaptists draw a pretty straight line from circumcision to baptism. Physical circumcision finds its new covenant fulfillment in baptism. But that's not the line the apostle Paul draws. Consider Colossians 2:11–12:

> You were also circumcised in Him with a circumcision not done with hands, by putting off the body of flesh, in the circumcision of the Messiah. Having been buried with Him in baptism, you were also raised with Him through faith in the working of God, who raised Him from the dead.

Paul says that Christians have been circumcised. How? Well, it was a circumcision done "without hands," that is, not by any human being. Who then circumcised us? It happened when we "put off the flesh," when we cast off our old, sinful nature. Who has the power to do that? Only God, of course. So we Christians were "circumcised" when God himself "cut off" our old selves, put to death our sinful nature, and gave us a new heart, a new spirit, a new self in Jesus. In other words, Paul is saying that all Christians have experienced the circumcision of the heart that God demanded of Israel and promised through the prophets.

What does this have to do with baptism? Paul says here that in baptism, we were buried and raised with Christ through faith. Because baptism is where faith goes public, Paul uses baptism as a shorthand reference to our whole conversion experience. When did we put off our old self? When we were buried and raised with Christ through faith. And baptism pictures this death and resurrection we undergo by faith.

So how does circumcision relate to baptism? Baptism is a new covenant sign of the circumcision of the heart, not of the flesh. Baptism signifies that the realities, which circumcision demanded but didn't guarantee, have now come true in a believer's life. Baptism says that what circumcision pointed toward but didn't possess has now come to pass. How is circumcision fulfilled in the new covenant? Not by baptizing babies, who don't yet—and may never—experience the realities of the new covenant. Instead, circumcision is fulfilled in the new covenant by the way baptism pictures the circumcision of the heart. Circumcision said to Israel, "Make yourselves new!" Baptism says to Christians, "This one has been made new!"

6. Paedobaptism makes God's new covenant promise less than a promise.

Finally, paedobaptism makes God's new covenant promise less than a promise. Paedobaptists are fond of quoting Acts 2:38–39, "For the promise is for you and for your children." But what promise are we talking about here? Paedobaptists say that God makes his new covenant promise to both believers and their children. And yet they also admit that many who are baptized as infants don't actually come to Christ. Many of those who receive the sign of the new covenant in infancy never experience the realities of the new covenant. In what sense, then, is God's new covenant promise actually a promise?

I'd argue that, according to paedobaptist practice, it isn't. To relieve this pressure, most Reformed paedobaptists, in one way or another, argue that there are two ways to belong to the new covenant—one external, one internal. In other words, you can be a member of the new covenant but not have your sins forgiven, not have God's law written on your heart, and not know the Lord. But as we've already seen, this divide between belonging to the covenant and fulfilling the covenant is exactly what God's new covenant promise erases. In the new covenant, God promises that all in the covenant will fulfill the covenant and experience its blessings, precisely because he will guarantee that they do. God himself will write his law on their hearts, grant them true knowledge of him, and forgive their sins (Jer. 31:31–34). The whole point of the new covenant is that to be in the covenant is to fulfill the covenant; to belong to the new covenant people is to have a new heart, a new self.

By including believers' infant children in the new covenant, paedobaptism makes God's new covenant promise less than a promise. Paedobaptism reverses the progress of redemptive history and inserts into the new covenant the very division that God destroyed—the gap between belonging to the covenant and fulfilling the covenant, being part of God's people and truly knowing God.

Paedobaptism invents the category "in the new covenant, but not of the new covenant." It makes God's promise less than a promise. Infant baptism is no guarantee that a child will grow up to know the Lord, as paedobaptists freely admit. But then what "promise" is God making to the children of believers? Not the new covenant promise. It's not a promise of God if it might not come true.

Responding to Paedobaptist Objections

Of course, paedobaptists offer counterarguments to the points I've made here. For the sake of thoroughness and fairness, let's consider five of them.[5]

1. The household baptisms in Acts show that in the new covenant God is still dealing with families as families.

Paedobaptists often point to the so-called "household baptisms" of Acts (e.g., Acts 16:15, 31–34; cf. 1 Cor. 1:16) to demonstrate that in the new covenant God is still dealing with families as families. If a whole household would be baptized when the head of the house came to faith, then surely that included infants. And even if it didn't, it shows that God's salvation works through families, not apart from them, so baptism should be given to believers' children.

So the argument goes. But what does the text actually say? Here's the account of Paul and Silas with the Philippian jailer:

> Then they spoke the message of the Lord to him along with everyone in his house. He took them the same hour of the night and washed their wounds. Right away he and all his family were baptized. He brought them into his house, set a meal before them, and rejoiced because he had believed God with his entire household. (Acts 16:32–34)

First, notice that Paul and Silas "spoke the message of the Lord" to everyone in the house. Whoever was in the house was old enough to be addressed by gospel preaching. This already tells against seeing infants or very young children present. Second, the jailer rejoiced because he had believed in God "with his entire household." The Greek adverb here meaning "with his entire household" could describe either the rejoicing or the believing, but the sense of the sentence probably requires both. The jailer's whole household rejoiced with him because they, like him, had heard the gospel, believed, and been baptized.

These verses in no way separate baptism from believing the gospel. They provide no warrant for extending the sign of the gospel to those who have not yet believed the gospel. And the more compressed account of Acts 16:15 should be read in light of the more detailed narrative here. Further, if these passages teach us to baptize members of a household who have not trusted in Christ, why don't most paedobaptists baptize the spouses of new believers, whether or not they have come to faith? And what about their teenage or adult children?

2. Paul tells children to obey their parents "in the Lord" (Eph. 6:1) and calls the children of a believing parent "holy" (1 Cor. 7:14). This assumes that they're covenant members.

In Ephesians 6:1 Paul tells children to obey their parents "in the Lord" (ESV), and in 1 Corinthians 7:14 he says that the children of a believing parent are "holy" (ESV), even if one parent is not a Christian. Doesn't this indicate that Paul views children as members of the new covenant?

Let's start with Ephesians 6:1. What does it mean that Paul addresses these children as being "in the Lord"? I think the Presbyterian New Testament scholar Frank Thielman offers a good answer. Throughout Ephesians this phrase refers to believers being united to Christ. Believers grow up into a holy temple "in the Lord" (2:21), the Ephesian Christians were formerly in darkness but became light "in the Lord" (5:8), and so on (cf. 4:1, 17). Why then does Paul speak to children in this way here? "Because they have been incorporated into Christ by faith (1:13), they should obey their parents."[6]

In other words, Paul is not addressing children as new covenant members who may or may not be united to Christ by faith. Instead, he addresses children as believers, and tells them to obey their parents as believers. He's simply not addressing the question of whether the as-yet-unbelieving children of believing parents have a special covenantal status.

In 1 Corinthians 7:14, Paul is counteracting the wrong idea that someone who is already married, then becomes a Christian, should separate from his or her unbelieving spouse. His rationale is, "For the unbelieving husband is made holy because of his wife, and the unbelieving wife is made holy because of her husband. Otherwise your children would be unclean, but as it is, they are holy" (ESV). Paedobaptists often infer from this reasoning that Paul views the children of a believing parent as "holy" because they are members of the new covenant, even though they don't necessarily experience the fulfillment of the new covenant's promises.

The first thing to note here is that the text says nothing explicit about baptism. Second, Paul describes the unbelieving spouse as "holy" in the same way as the children. So again, any argument for infant baptism here must also be an argument for non-believing adult baptism! Very few paedobaptists take that step, so their argument from this verse is flatly inconsistent.

3. In Romans 4:11, Paul says that Abraham received the sign of circumcision as a seal of righteousness by faith.

In Romans 4:11 Paul says that Abraham "received the sign of circumcision as a seal of the righteousness that he had by faith while still uncircumcised. This was to make him the father of all who believe but are not circumcised, so that righteousness may be credited to them also."

So Paul teaches that the sign of circumcision was, for Abraham, a seal of the righteousness he had by faith before he was circumcised. Paedobaptists point out that Abraham's descendants, who were circumcised at eight days old, received this "seal" of righteousness-by-faith before they ever came to share Abraham's faith and the righteousness that comes by faith. In other words, God commanded Abraham to extend the "objective" sign of circumcision regardless of whether the subjective reality of righteousness-by-faith was present. Further, paedobaptists argue that baptism and circumcision signify essentially the same reality: circumcision signified righteousness-by-faith, and baptism signifies union with Christ, in whom we are righteous by faith. Therefore, just like circumcision, baptism should be applied to the children of covenant members as an "objective" sign of union with Christ whether or not the subjective reality of faith is or ever will be present.

But this is simply not the point Paul is making in this passage. Paul's point is the order of righteousness and circumcision: Abraham was righteous by faith *before* being circumcised. Genesis 15 comes before Genesis 17. Paul makes this point to underscore the reality that Abraham is the "father of all who believe without being circumcised" (Rom. 4:11). In other words, uncircumcised Gentiles who come to faith in Christ are declared righteous by faith just as Abraham was. They don't need to be circumcised in order to receive God's covenant blessings, because Abraham himself was uncircumcised when he received righteousness by faith.

In other words, Paul is talking about Abraham's circumcision, not everyone else's. He's talking about what it meant for God to declare Abraham righteous before giving him the covenant of circumcision. Paul is not teaching that circumcision inherently signifies righteousness-by-faith; instead, he's teaching that the sign of circumcision was a seal of *Abraham's* righteousness-by-faith. God gave Abraham circumcision as a confirmation of the right standing before God that he already had. Paul's point is not what circumcision signifies for all who receive it, but what God was saying to Abraham by giving him circumcision.

Finally, the passage nowhere mentions baptism or connects baptism to circumcision. It neither asserts nor assumes that baptism and circumcision signify the same realities and should be administered in the same manner.

4. To reject paedobaptism is to kick children out of the church.

Paedobaptists say that God included the children of believers among his people under the old covenant, so to refuse to baptize infants is to kick children out of the church. But this begs the question of what the church is and how God forms it. If God forms his church by bringing his new covenant promises into effect in people's lives, then unbelieving children aren't "in" the church—the universal body of Christ, those united to Christ by faith—whether we baptize them or not. Paedobaptists say that those who don't baptize infants have taken children who should be in and put them out, but they've taken those who are still out and put them in.

And of course the children of believers should be included in the life of the church in the sense of worshiping with the church, being taught by the church, and growing into ever-deeper experiences of fellowship in the church. Baptists as much as paedobaptists believe that we're called to raise our children "in the training and instruction of the Lord" (Eph. 6:4). Being trained and instructed in the Lord involves participating deeply in the life of the church, in ways appropriate to a child's age, maturity, and spiritual state.

5. To reject paedobaptism is to fracture the unity of Scripture and of God's plan of salvation.

Paedobaptists love to accent the unity and continuity of God's plan of salvation. They love to highlight the threads that draw the whole Bible to that. And together every Christian should say "Amen!" There is one God. He has one plan of salvation. He is gathering one people together out of every nation, who are saved through the one offering of Jesus Christ and who inherit all God's promises in him.

But every Christian also has to deal with the discontinuities in God's plan of salvation. We no longer offer sacrifices in a temple in Jerusalem. We are no longer bound by God's law to maintain ritual purity, abstain from foods proscribed by the Mosaic law, and so on. Every Christian has to balance the continuities and discontinuities between the old covenant and the new. If some Christians insisted that believers circumcise their children in obedience to the Mosaic law, how would paedobaptist Christians respond? Along with the apostle Paul, they would insist that such believers are turning back the clock of redemptive history and erasing the discontinuities between how God worked in the old covenant and in the new.

Everyone sees both continuity and discontinuity between the old covenant and the new. The trick is getting the balance right. And I would argue, and have argued in this chapter, that to baptize infants is to assert continuity where the new covenant itself insists on discontinuity. To baptize infants is to bring over from the old covenant to the new the very structure that the new covenant dismantles.

Just Doesn't Fit

What does all this add up to? Simply that infant baptism is not what the Bible means by baptism. The Bible neither commands nor implicitly authorizes churches to baptize infants. As plausible as the covenantal paedobaptist argument is, it just doesn't fit with what Scripture teaches about baptism and the new covenant. Infant baptism isn't baptism.

So if you were "baptized" as an infant, I hope you've come to understand from the Bible why that "baptism" wasn't really baptism at all. It's not that infant baptism is somewhat faulty, like a car with a bad alternator that still manages to chug along. Instead, infant baptism simply isn't baptism. Those who were "baptized" as infants haven't actually been baptized, so they still need to be.

Some who come to this understanding are still hesitant to be baptized, though, because they would see getting baptized as a criticism of their parents—or at least, they fear their parents might see it that way. Certainly we must honor our parents and express any theological disagreement with them gently and humbly. But Jesus alone commands our ultimate obedience. If Jesus understands baptism differently than our own parents do, then it's Jesus we need to obey rather than them (Luke 14:26).

CHAPTER 4

Why Is Baptism Required for Church Membership?

Some of you may be reading this book because you want to join a church and you have to be baptized in order to join. But why do churches require baptism for membership in the first place? Is that really a biblical practice? Won't that exclude some true Christians from membership, since not all Christians agree about what counts as baptism?

This chapter addresses all these questions by presenting a biblical case for why baptism is required for church membership. To be clear, by "baptism" I mean the baptism of a believer, not an infant. As we saw in the previous chapter, infant "baptism" simply is not baptism.

This chapter is also addressed to church leaders, those who have the most immediate influence over whether their church will require baptism for membership. My goal is to persuade you that you should. I'll make the case in seven steps, then address the strongest objection.[7]

Seven Reasons Why Baptism Is Required for Church Membership

There's no proof-text that speaks directly and definitively to this issue. So in order to discern why baptism is required for church membership, we need to weigh up and weave together lots of biblical material. This chapter will get a bit technical at times, but the argument here simply deepens and unpacks the definition of baptism we explored in chapter 1. Here then are seven factors that, taken together, demonstrate that the Bible makes baptism a requirement for church membership.

1. Baptism is where faith goes public.

Remember the definition of baptism we set out in chapter 1: *baptism is a church's act of affirming and portraying a believer's union with Christ by immersing him or her in water, and a believer's act of publicly committing him or herself to Christ and his people, thereby uniting a believer to the church and marking off him or her from the world.*

In other words, baptism is where faith goes public. The Christian life is a life of public witness to Christ (Matt. 10:32–33), and that witness begins at baptism. At Pentecost those converted by Peter's preaching stepped out from the crowd, declaring allegiance to Christ as Lord and Savior by submitting to baptism (Acts 2:38–41). In baptism we "out" ourselves as Christians. We publicly identify with the crucified and resurrected Christ and with his people.

As we've seen, Jesus commanded his disciples to make disciples by preaching the gospel to them, baptizing them, and teaching them to obey everything he commanded (Matt. 28:19). So it's no surprise that at Pentecost Peter commanded his hearers, "Repent and be baptized every one of you in the name of Jesus Christ for the forgiveness of your sins" (Acts 2:38 ESV). If you claim to follow Christ, this is the first of his commands that you must obey. After trusting Christ, baptism is the first thing a new believer does. If you haven't been baptized, you've not yet crossed off the first item on Jesus' discipleship to-do list.

Why is baptism required for church membership? Because baptism is where faith goes public. It's where invisible faith first becomes visible. It's how a new Christian shows up on the church's and the world's radar. This is the seed from which the following reasons grow.

2. Baptism is the initiating oath-sign of the new covenant.

Since baptism is how a believer commits him or herself to Christ and his people, baptism is also the initiating oath-sign of the new covenant. It is the act that publicly enacts one's promise to trust in Christ and live out the new covenant.

Through his death, Jesus inaugurated the promised new covenant, as we discussed in the last chapter (Jer. 31:31–34; Luke 22:19–20; Heb. 8:1–13). All covenants are ratified by an oath: a solemn, self-obligating promise. Yet an oath isn't just something spoken, it can be acted too, or active instead. When God made a covenant with Abraham, he passed between the halves of slaughtered animals (Gen. 15:1–21). This oath-sign ratified God's promise to Abraham and signified that if God proved unfaithful to his covenant, he himself would bear judgment. In the death of Jesus, God the Son did bear judgment—not for his unfaithfulness, but for ours. The new covenant was ratified when Jesus himself paid the ultimate price for our sins (Heb. 9:15).

The old covenant had circumcision, an oath-sign which ratified an individual's entrance into the covenant. So also the new covenant comes with an oath-sign—actually two of them. The first, baptism, is its initiating oath-sign. It is a solemn, symbolic vow that ratifies one's entrance into the new covenant. In baptism we appeal to God to accept us on the terms of his new covenant (1 Pet. 3:21), and we pledge ourselves to fulfill, by grace, all that his new covenant requires of us (Matt. 28:19). In baptism we own God as our God, and he owns us as his people. In baptism we swear the vow, "Do you take this Jesus to be your Lord and Savior?" "I do."

So when the church asks, "Who belongs to the new covenant?" one part of the answer is, "Who has sworn the oath?" That is, who has been baptized? Just like a soldier can't take up arms until he has sworn allegiance to his country, you cannot enter the fellowship of the new covenant until you have sworn the covenant oath. The church is where the new covenant shows up on earth, and baptism is how an individual shows up as a new covenant member. Baptism is necessary for church membership because baptism is the initiating oath-sign of the new covenant.

3. Baptism is the passport of the kingdom and the kingdom citizen's swearing-in ceremony.

Third, baptism is the passport of the kingdom and the kingdom citizen's swearing-in ceremony. As we saw in chapter 1, when Jesus inaugurated the kingdom of heaven on earth, he established the church as an embassy of that kingdom. He gave the church the "keys of the kingdom" in order to identify its citizens before the world by affirming the professions of those who credibly confess faith in him (Matt. 16:19; 18:18–19). And the initial and initiating means by which the church identifies individuals as kingdom citizens is baptism (Matt. 28:19). Baptism is how a church declares, "This one belongs to Jesus."

Baptism is the passport of the kingdom. We become kingdom citizens by faith in the king, and in baptism the church recognizes and affirms our citizenship. And baptism enables other embassies of the kingdom—other local churches—to recognize us as kingdom citizens.

From another angle, baptism is a kingdom citizen's swearing-in ceremony. It's how we formally take up our new office of representing Christ and his kingdom on earth. Therefore, in order for a church to recognize someone as a kingdom citizen, that citizen needs to produce his or her passport. Baptism is necessary for church membership because it's the passport of the kingdom and the kingdom citizen's swearing-in ceremony.

4. Baptism is a necessary criterion by which a church recognizes who is a Christian.

A fourth reason why baptism is necessary for church membership is an implication of our first three points. Because baptism is how a church publicly identifies someone as a Christian, it's also a necessary criterion by which a church recognizes who is a Christian. Identification is for recognition. The Louisville Cardinals wear red so they can recognize each other on the court when they're trouncing the blue-jerseyed Kentucky Wildcats. And baptism is the team jersey of Christianity.

Baptism is therefore a necessary, though not sufficient, criterion by which the church is to recognize Christians. It's not enough for someone to claim to be a Christian, or for everyone in the church to think someone is a Christian; Jesus has bound the church's judgment to baptism. Jesus gave us baptism, in part, so we can tell each other apart from the world. By publicly identifying people as Christians, baptism draws a line between the church and the world. Baptism marks off Christians as Christians, which means baptism is necessary for church membership. A church simply isn't authorized to recognize someone as a member of Jesus' team until that person puts on the jersey.

5. Baptism is an effective sign of church membership.

Fifth, baptism is an effective sign of church membership. This is also an inference from our first three points. If baptism is where faith goes public, the initiating oath-sign of the new covenant, the passport of the kingdom, and a kingdom citizen's swearing-in ceremony, then baptism is an effective sign of church membership. It creates the churchly reality to which it points: a Christian belonging to a local church, and that local church affirming a Christian's profession and uniting him or her to itself.

If membership is a house, baptism is the front door. By stepping through the front door you enter the house. Normally, therefore, baptism isn't just a precursor to church membership; it confers church membership. Baptism begins church membership. For a new convert, baptism is the New Testament way to join a church. Because baptism is an effective sign of church membership, baptism is necessary for church membership.

6. The Lord's Supper is the other effective sign of church membership.

In point two we saw that the new covenant comes with two signs. The first is baptism, its initiating oath-sign. The second is the Lord's Supper, which is its renewing oath-sign. When we partake together of the bread and the cup, we commit ourselves anew to Christ and his new covenant.

Yet this isn't something we do as individuals, but as a church (1 Cor. 11:17–18, 20, 33–34). And partaking of the Lord's Supper entails responsibility for the church. To eat and drink in a way that despises the body negates the Lord's Supper and incurs God's judgment (1 Cor. 11:27, 29). Therefore, just as we pledge ourselves to Christ in the Lord's Supper, so we also pledge ourselves to each other. In the same act in which we again own Jesus as our Savior, we own each other as brothers and sisters.

This means that the Lord's Supper is the other effective sign of church membership. As Paul says, "Because there is one bread, we who are many are one body, for all of us share that one bread" (1 Cor. 10:17). The Lord's Supper doesn't just represent our unity, it ratifies and seals it. Because it enacts our fellowship with each other, the Lord's Supper makes many one. This is why church membership is first and foremost inclusion at the Table, and church discipline is first and foremost exclusion from the Table.

Baptism is required for church membership because you can't participate in the renewing oath-sign of the covenant until you've performed its initiating oath-sign. You can't participate in the family meal of the Lord's Supper until you've entered the house through the front door of baptism.

7. Without baptism, membership doesn't exist.

What does all this add up to? Simply this: we can't remove baptism from what's required for church membership because without baptism, membership doesn't actually exist. "Membership" is a theological term for the relation between a Christian and a church, which the ordinances imply and normally create. This relation of church membership is evident in the New Testament in that some people are "inside" the church and others are "outside" (1 Cor. 5:12).

Baptism and the Lord's Supper ratify the covenant relation which is church membership. Therefore, there is no such thing as membership without baptism. To speak of membership without baptism is like speaking of a marriage without vows. Marriage is a covenant relation constituted by vows; membership is a covenant relation constituted by the oath-signs of baptism and the Lord's Supper. You can't have the relation without the oath that constitutes it. Therefore, you can't have membership without baptism.

The fact that the ordinances are effective signs of church membership reminds us to keep our understanding of church membership and the ordinances tightly tied together. When our concept of the church membership is not tightly integrated with the ordinances, our ideas about church membership have become unbiblical. In Scripture, church membership describes the relationship which the ordinances create.

But Won't This Exclude True Christians from Membership?

This means that churches should require all those who wish to join their membership to be baptized—that is, baptized as believers. But doesn't this mean that some genuine Christians will be excluded from membership, particularly those who regard their infant "baptism" as biblical baptism?

Many Christians take it for granted that a church should never exclude someone from membership whom they're confident is a Christian. And I think that is almost exactly right. But the problem is, baptism fits within the box marked "How a Church Knows Someone Is a Christian." Baptism isn't a separate requirement for church membership in addition to a credible profession of faith; it is *how* someone publicly professes faith.

Therefore, baptism is a necessary but not sufficient factor in how a church is to know who is a Christian in the first place. All the members of a church might be convinced that a certain unbaptized person is a Christian, but Jesus has bound the church's judgment—and the formal, public affirmation of membership—to baptism. Jesus has given the church no authority to affirm someone's faith until that faith is publicly professed in baptism.

Because of all that baptism is and does, a church is simply not authorized to extend the relation of membership to those who have not performed its effective sign. A church may not admit to the renewing oath-sign of the new covenant anyone who has not performed its initiating oath-sign. To do so would be to depart from Jesus' own appointed means for marking off his people from the world and binding them to each other. Baptism draws the line between the church and the world. We are not at liberty to draw it elsewhere.

Imagine you go to board an airplane, but instead of bringing your boarding pass to the gate you leave it at the security checkpoint. When the gate agent asks for your boarding pass, what will happen? If you tell him that you used to have the boarding pass but already handed it in, that won't get you anywhere. The gate agent needs to see the pass in order to let you on the plane. He simply isn't authorized to admit you otherwise. A boarding pass is what identifies you as a passenger on the flight; baptism is what identifies you as a Christian, and therefore as qualified to join a church.

As the nineteenth-century Baptist theologian John Dagg put it, "As profession is necessary to church-membership, so is baptism, which is the appointed ceremony of profession. Profession is the substance, and baptism is the form; but Christ's command requires the form as well as the substance."[8] Paedobaptists are denied membership because they lack not the substance of a credible profession but its form. Thinking you've been baptized, even on the basis of a sophisticated, widely held interpretation of Scripture, does not mean you've been baptized. And a church is no more free to admit an unbaptized person to membership than a gate agent is to admit someone onto a plane without a boarding pass.

It is troubling to exclude from membership a faithful, godly, paedobaptist Christian. But it should be more troubling to revise the role Christ has assigned to baptism, to make one of his commands optional, and to undermine his authority in the church. It should be more troubling to allow a Christian—however sincere in his or her error—to continue in disobedience to Christ, and to add the church's approval to that disobedience. It should be more troubling to allow the public profession of the gospel to be privatized. It should be more troubling to try to gather the church by setting aside the very ordinance Jesus has appointed for that purpose.

Drawing Lines

Jesus appointed baptism, in part, to mark off his people from the world. Baptism and the Lord's Supper picture, promote, and preserve the gospel by publicly identifying Christ's people.

Baptism displays our death to sin and our resurrection to new life in Christ. It seals our commitment to Christ and his people. It draws a line between the church and the world, extending the invitation, "Look, world: see what a gospel people are like!"

And because baptism draws a line between the church and the world, it also draws a line around the church. Baptism binds one to many. It adds a believer to the public company of the people of God on earth. Baptism is therefore an effective sign of church membership. Baptism doesn't just mark the way into the church; instead, baptism is itself the front door. Normally, baptism confers church membership.

For all these reasons, baptism is required for church membership. Maybe you're interested in joining a church but have been put off by the requirement to be baptized first. If so, I hope you've now seen that Jesus not only requires you to be baptized, but he also requires his church to require you to be baptized. And if you're a church leader, I hope you've seen that your church should require those who claim Christ as their Savior to be baptized—just like Jesus does.

CHAPTER 5

When Is "Baptism" Not Baptism?

My younger daughter is utterly, adorably obsessed with dinosaurs. Often the first thing she says in the morning is, "D'you wanna play dinos wif me?" At night she sometimes brings a large plastic Triceratops with her to bed, above which hangs a poster filled with dinosaurs' pictures and names. She's only two and a half, but she can recognize dozens of species, telling them apart by their crests or plates or tails. If you ask her, say, "Is that one a Brachiosaurus?" she might reply, "No, dat's an Apatosaurus! Brachiosaurus has a longer neck."

To say what something is, you have to be able to say what it isn't. The past three chapters have mainly focused on what baptism is; now we turn to what it isn't. The reason for this is twofold. First, given how we've defined baptism, some readers who think they've been baptized might now be wondering if they really have been. Second, church leaders in particular will often have to make a judgment as to whether what a prospective member is calling "baptism" really was. So we're going to survey four of the most common scenarios in which "baptism" isn't actually baptism.

If You Were "Baptized" as an Infant

We saw in chapter 3 that infant "baptism" isn't actually baptism. However well-intentioned those Christians are who practice infant baptism, and however sophisticated their biblical rationale for it, the Bible simply does not authorize us to baptize the infant children of believers. Baptism is a sign that the gospel has taken effect in someone's life, that a person *is* united to Christ. Baptism points to a promise fulfilled.

So if you were "baptized" as an infant, you still need to be baptized—for the first time. Despite the noble intentions of the church that "baptized" you, you remain in the same position as anyone else who came to Christ and has not yet been baptized.

If You Were Baptized as a "Believer" but Not a Believer

Some people are baptized of their own accord, treating the act as a profession of faith in Christ, but later realize they weren't Christians at all at the time of their baptism. Consider the following scenario:

> I was baptized at the age of 13 before I was really walking with the Lord. It came as a result of covering the topic in a youth Bible class after which we were asked if we would like to be baptized; and considering the majority of the class was doing it, I decided to as well. I recall at the time being too embarrassed to even tell my school friends about it, never mind ask them to come.
>
> The Lord really worked in my life at the age of 20, and that's when I would say he really opened my eyes to what following Jesus was all about. Ideally that's when I would have been baptized, but obviously I already had been. I'd be interested to hear your thoughts on getting baptized for a second time and if you feel that would be necessary.[9]

So this person—for convenience let's assume it's a man—doesn't think he was a Christian when he was baptized. It happened "before I was really walking with the Lord." His motive for being baptized was to go along with the crowd: "the majority of the class was doing it." Far from treating baptism as an opportunity to publicly pledge himself to Christ before any and all who care to know, he tried to keep it as quiet as possible, not telling any of his school friends. And from what his narrative tells us, it sounds like he came to a true understanding of discipleship to Jesus, and truly trusted in Jesus, several years later.

So, should this person be baptized again, a second time? No, of course not. He should be baptized—for the first time. Once you've been baptized, you've been baptized. But if you were not a Christian at the time of your "baptism"—if, to the best of your knowledge, your "baptism" was not a genuine profession of trust in Christ and a sincere pledge of submission to Christ—then your "baptism" wasn't baptism. If this describes you, you need to be baptized.

But there's another scenario we need to discuss. Consider this young woman's (imaginary, but very common) story:

> I grew up in a Christian home. My parents taught me the gospel, and when I was six years old I prayed with my dad to receive Christ. I remember feeling convicted of my sin and knowing that Jesus died on the cross to save me. I was baptized a few months later. From that point on, I always considered myself a Christian, and I knew that meant trusting in Jesus and living by his Word.
>
> But in my teen years I went through a period of doubt. I began to have questions about whether the Bible was true, and I didn't always like what it said. When I prayed, it didn't always feel like God was there. I didn't go through any huge rebellion, but sometimes my life looked more like my non-Christian friends' than what a Christian is supposed to live like. Sometimes I cheated on tests at school, and a few times I lied to my parents about where I was going at night so they wouldn't know I was out drinking with my friends.

Now I'm twenty and I'm not really sure when I became a Christian. In the past couple years I feel like my faith has really come alive and I've grown spiritually more than I did in the ten years before that. Since I don't really know if I was a Christian when I was baptized, shouldn't I get baptized now, just to be sure?

This situation is a lot messier. On the one hand, this young woman was baptized as a response to hearing and apparently believing the gospel. And there seemed to be some spiritual fruit in her life early on. But what do we make of those teen years? She didn't stop calling herself a Christian, but was she really living as a Christian? And now that she's more mature, she has a tough time thinking that her younger self really trusted in Christ, given her mixed track record. So what should she do?

I'd argue that a person who was previously baptized as a profession of faith in Christ should only be "re-baptized" if she is strongly convinced that she was not a Christian at that time. Ultimately, that's a judgment someone has to make, him or herself, with the help of godly church leaders. Baptism is meant to be done once and shouldn't be repeated over mere doubts.

In this case, it sounds like the young woman genuinely understood and embraced the gospel at a young age. Even in those mixed teen years, she never abandoned herself to a lifestyle characterized by unrepentant sin, and she never renounced her faith in Christ. It's all too easy, in retrospect, to mistake childlike faith for no faith at all, and to impose an adult standard of spiritual fruit on a child or even a teenager. This would be a different conversation if at some point she had denied the faith or had immersed herself in serious, public, unrepentant sin. As it is, I think she should probably treat her earlier profession as sincere; but again, that's a judgment she has to make for herself. I think she should seek baptism—and the church should baptize her—if and only if she is positively convinced that she was not a Christian when she was baptized.

If the Church That Baptized You Denies the Gospel

Baptism is an emblem of the gospel. It dramatically depicts the good news of Jesus Christ finding and freeing a sinner. To be baptized is to be identified with Jesus and his saving work. Baptism therefore depends on the gospel—no gospel, no baptism.

If every Christian were authorized to baptize simply by being a Christian, the church wouldn't factor into this equation. But since Jesus has authorized the church to make official declarations on earth on behalf of heaven, then, under normal circumstances, only the church is authorized to baptize. And only a body of believers that affirms and proclaims the gospel has a right to call itself a church.

Sometimes assemblies of professing Christians call themselves "churches" but have so departed from the truth of the gospel that they effectively deny it. For instance, if a church teaches that Jesus' death was merely a display of God's yearning love for mankind, and his resurrection wasn't a bodily event but a spiritual impression in the hearts of his disciples, that church has replaced the gospel with a false gospel. And as Paul says, anything but the true, apostolic gospel is no gospel at all (Gal. 1:6–7).

Some churches effectively deny the gospel by their beliefs about baptism itself. For instance, if a church treats baptism as saving, as that which grants forgiveness and new birth, then that church has actually put baptism in the place of the gospel. Baptism and the gospel should be inseparable: everyone who believes is commanded to be baptized, and baptism attests and broadcasts the gospel. But baptism should not be identified with, or mistaken for, the gospel.

A church that effectively denies the gospel is no church at all, which means they have no authorization from Jesus to baptize people in his name. Therefore a "baptism" performed by a gospel-denying church is not in fact baptism.

If this scenario hits home, how can you determine if the church that baptized you does in fact deny the gospel? It's complicated. If you have any inkling that this might be the case for you, I'd encourage you to ask the leaders of the church you currently attend to help you work through it.

To be clear: no church has perfect doctrine, and no preacher is infallible. I'm not saying a baptism is only valid if a church is 100 percent doctrinally sound. And I'm not saying that if a pastor himself proves unfaithful to the gospel he preaches, the baptisms he performed are rendered invalid. Instead, I'm saying that the same gospel that gives birth to the church in the first place is what gives authority to baptize and be baptized. I'm less interested in the man doing the baptizing than in the church authorizing it. In order for a church to baptize, it must affirm and proclaim the biblical gospel.

If the Baptism Has No Connection Whatsoever to a Church

The last situation we'll consider is the hardest of all to pin down: a baptism performed with no connection whatsoever to a church. Let's work our way in from two extremes. On one end, you have a baptism performed by a pastor in a gathering of a gospel-preaching church. No problem there. On the other end, let's update our dunking scenario from chapter 1. You're in a friend's backyard pool at a casual summer get-together. You're both believers—in fact, your friend led you to Christ just a few weeks prior.

He says, "Hey, you haven't been baptized yet, have you?"

"Nope. I guess I should be."

"Why not do it now? I can baptize you."

"Um, okay."

If at that point your friend dips you under the water and says the words, "I baptize you in the name of the Father, and of the Son, and of the Holy Spirit," have you been baptized? Unlike in the dunking scene of chapter 1, you're acting willingly. You did in fact recently come to faith in Christ. And your friend knows you've trusted in Christ since he's the one who preached the gospel to you. But do these factors add up to baptism?

I'd suggest that in most circumstances, the answer is no. Remember that in baptism, a person commits himself to Christ and his people, and a church affirms a believer's profession of faith. But there's no sense in which your friend is acting on behalf of a church. There's no sense in which the church is speaking to you in Jesus' name when your friend dunks you under water. That is the decisive problem here, the missing piece keeping this scenario from qualifying as baptism.

However, I did say "most circumstances." If you're in a place where there is no church because there are no Christians, I would argue that anyone who has the gospel has the authority to baptize. If there isn't yet a local church, then every Christian, as it were, carries the seed of the church with him—that seed being the gospel, which is sown through proclamation. We'll talk more about this in the next chapter. For now, my point is simply that where no church yet exists, whoever preaches the gospel can and should baptize those who respond to the gospel.

But in the pool-dunking story, that's not the case. There are plenty of churches around. Your friend, as it happens, is a member of one. So, instead of taking the oversight of your discipleship into his own hands, he should commit you to the church's care. When you come to Christ, he should say, "Great, now let me introduce you to Christ's people. There are some other faithful churches in our city, but this is the body I belong to. Let's talk to the church's pastors about what it would look like for you to get baptized and join the church."

Again, in an area where a local church exists, a baptism with no connection whatsoever to a church isn't baptism. Remember, baptism is a statement by two parties, not one—the baptizer and the baptizee. And since a church exists here, but a church has in no way spoken on behalf of Jesus, this dunking simply doesn't qualify as baptism. Only the church is authorized to swear in kingdom citizens. Only the church is authorized to administer the initiating oath-sign of the new covenant. Only the church has the authority to say, "Look here, every-body: this one belongs to Jesus."

What does it mean for a baptism to be connected to a local church? We'll look more at this in the next chapter, but to preview, I think there's real flexibility here. I don't think Scripture mandates that a pastor be the one to baptize, though I think it's normally wise. I don't think Scripture mandates that baptism be performed in whole-church gatherings. Though again, I think that's wise and that it best fits with baptism's role as commitment to the body and affirmation by the body. So if baptism doesn't have to be performed by a pastor, in a church gathering, that leaves quite a bit of flexibility in how baptism may legitimately be administered.

Still, I'm saying that where a church exists, there's a line between a baptism that is somehow tied to a church, and therefore valid, and a baptism that is in no way tied to a church, and therefore invalid. Some cases are pretty clear one way or the other. But not all. For example, a close friend of mine actually was baptized by a friend, in a swimming pool. They were at a Christian camp together, and lots of people were being baptized. Is this a valid baptism? I'm not sure. If I remember correctly, the camp had some kind of oversight by a local church, but I don't know how involved the church was or wasn't in those camp baptisms. This case seems right on the line. Since the context was public, not private, and since there was some, albeit distant, connection to a church, I'd be inclined to give it the benefit of the doubt. But it's far from clear, and I can easily see how a church would come to the opposite conclusion.

Ultimately, these are the kinds of judgments local churches need to make when they assess candidates for baptism. On the one hand, we don't want to set up stricter standards than Scripture. On the other, we don't want to allow baptism to become privatized and severed from the church, robbing the ordinance of its disciple-marking, line-drawing, church-forming role. This calls for wisdom and biblical insight.

This also calls for discernment among individual Christians. If you've recently come to Christ, or recently led someone to Christ, make sure your first stop in discipleship is the church. The church is the body Jesus has appointed to act and speak on his behalf, representing his heavenly kingdom on earth. And the church is the place where disciples all grow together into the fullness of Christ (Eph. 4:11–16). Where does a new Christian go his first day on the job? The local church.

Next and Last

This chapter has focused on what baptism isn't in order to provide a clearer picture of what it is. If your own experience fits with any of the scenarios we've discussed in this chapter, I hope you've come away with a clearer sense that you've either already fulfilled Jesus' command to be baptized, or that you haven't yet, and you need to. And if you're a church leader, I hope you've developed some clearer categories for what your church will, and won't, recognize as baptism.

But of course, churches don't just recognize baptisms, they also baptize people. So in our next, and last, chapter we turn to the question, "How should churches practice baptism?"

CHAPTER 6

How Should Churches Practice Baptism?

For most Christians, the main thing they have to do with baptism is get baptized. Certainly we should reflect on our baptism to remind us that we've been united to Christ, and that now we're both empowered and commanded to live a new life (Rom. 6:1–4). And as we have opportunity, we should encourage and exhort other Christians who haven't been baptized to do so. But as far as your own obedience to Jesus is concerned, once you've been baptized, that's all there is to it.

For church leaders, it's a different story. Most gospel-preaching churches regularly have the opportunity to baptize new believers, and it's typically church leaders who do the baptizing. But the actual practice of baptism raises a host of questions: How much water needs to be used? Is pouring or sprinkling as good as immersing? Who should do the baptizing? How does baptism relate to church membership? When and where should churches baptize? How soon after coming to Christ should someone be baptized?

This chapter addresses all these questions, in the order I just listed them. To put it in shorthand, we're going to consider baptism's mode, administrator, result, context, and timing.

I hope that even those who aren't church leaders will feel the relevance of these questions. If you haven't been baptized, this chapter can help you sort out how and where to seek baptism. If you have been baptized, this chapter can help you help others get baptized in a way that accords with Scripture.

Finally, a word to those who are or someday may be missionaries, preaching the gospel in a context where no church yet exists. Since my counsel in this chapter assumes the existence of a church, it doesn't apply to the very first baptisms performed in a location just being reached by the gospel. But if you're obeying the Great Commission and teaching Jesus' disciples to obey all he commanded, then you will teach all your converts, including the very first from the very beginning, that following Jesus means forming a church. Jesus says, "For where two or three are gathered together in My name, I am there among them" (Matt. 18:20). This means that as soon as you have more than one new believer in Jesus, you have the makings of a church, and you should lead those believers to make a church. Almost as soon as these new believers come to Christ, they should be involved, as a church, in overseeing the baptism of new believers. So this chapter is just as relevant to missionaries as it is to leaders of established churches.

Mode

How much water do churches need in order to baptize someone? Should they build or borrow spaces big enough to dunk people, or is a baptismal font or pitcher enough?

In chapter 1 we saw that the Greek word for *baptize* means to plunge or immerse under water. John baptized people in Aenon because there was much water there (John 3:23), and the Ethiopian eunuch asked to be baptized when he spotted a roadside pond (Acts 8:36). And for this baptism, the Ethiopian eunuch and Philip "went down" into the water and then "came up" out of it (Acts 8:38–39). It's theoretically possible that they went into the water and then Philip cupped water in his hands and poured it over his companion, but that's highly unlikely. It doesn't explain why the eunuch appealed for baptism precisely when he saw a large body of water. And why would both men go through the trouble of either undressing or soaking their clothes if a full dunking were unnecessary?

Further, immersion best captures the symbolism of being buried and raised with Christ. In both Romans 6:1–4 and Colossians 2:11–12 Paul takes for granted that baptism signifies this union with Christ's death, burial, and resurrection. The most reasonable inference is that his readers would call to mind a time not when they were sprinkled or doused with water, but when they were thrust under it and pulled up out of it.

So I would argue that the Bible presents immersion as the normative mode of baptism. This isn't just something the early Christians did that we should feel free to abandon. Instead, the mode of baptism is bound up with the symbolism and significance of the rite; so churches should take whatever steps necessary to be able to baptize believers by immersion.

Administrator

Next, who should do the baptizing? If baptism is an act of the church, then its administrator should be authorized by the church. One who performs baptism should act on behalf of the church, not his own initiative or authority.

The church as a whole exercises the keys of the kingdom (Matt. 16:19; 18:19), but only one person baptizes. Yet baptism is an exercise of the keys of the kingdom. It's a church's official affirmation of someone's claim to follow Christ. In baptism, the church speaks for Jesus, so the baptizer needs to speak for the church.

Pastors, also called "elders" or "overseers" in Scripture (e.g., 1 Tim. 3:1; 5:17), are appointed by the church to teach the church and lead the church. They're recognized by the church to exercise oversight over the church. They teach the Word, exhort the church to obey the Word, model faithfulness to the Word, and direct the life of the church in accordance with the Word. I would suggest, therefore, that while

Scripture does not require baptism to be performed by a pastor, it normally should be. Pastors or elders are those who already act on behalf of the church as they teach the Word, and baptism is a public rite of response to the Word that visibly proclaims the Word. I don't think this means that only the "senior pastor" should baptize; instead I think every pastor or elder is authorized to do so.

As I said, I don't think that having a pastor baptize is an absolute requirement. Nevertheless if a church is inclined to authorize others to baptize, I think they should carefully consider who, and why, and how. For instance, if a church regularly allows fathers to baptize their own children, that may subtly send the misleading message that baptism is an ordinance of the family, not of the church.

But the most important point here is that baptism is an act of the church, not an individual Christian, which means its administrator must be authorized by the church. Individual Christians do not have the authority to baptize simply by being Christians.

As I said in the previous chapter, where no church yet exists, the situation is different. If you're the only Christian in a city, you *are* the church in that city. So it's not exactly that you're acting on your own initiative apart from a church's authorization. Instead, you are carrying, and hopefully sowing, the seed of the church—the gospel. Where the gospel seed bears fruit in faith and repentance, you should ratify that response in baptism. And as soon as you have two or three who can gather in Jesus' name, you should instruct the new church that baptism is an act they are ultimately responsible to perform and oversee. And you should perform future baptisms under their oversight and on their behalf.

Result

Baptism is a church's act of affirming and portraying a believer's union with Christ by immersing him or her in water, and a believer's act of publicly committing him or herself to Christ and his people, thereby uniting a believer to the church and marking off him or her from the world. In baptism, a believer commits to God's people and God's people commit to that believer. Therefore, where a church exists, baptism should confer church membership. The church doing the baptizing should, by that very act, be inducting this new believer into their number. Baptism isn't just a prerequisite to church membership; normally, baptism begins church membership. Church membership is the house, and baptism is the front door.

The only legitimate exception that I can see is when a new believer is immediately moving to an area where, as far as anyone knows, no church exists. For example, a brand-new Christian who serves in the Navy might be heading out to spend a year living on a ship. Or someone who works for an international business may be moving to the Middle East and have no idea whether a church exists in their future city. Such situations aren't ideal, but sometimes they're unavoidable. These new believers find themselves in Ethiopian eunuch-like territory. So in these truly exceptional circumstances, a church should baptize them, pray for them, send them off, and encourage them to find whatever Christian fellowship they can during their sojourn abroad. And we've already addressed a frontier missionary situation. The first new convert in a region isn't baptized into a church, but as soon as one or two others are baptized they should form a church together.

In every other case, baptism and church membership should be inseparable. No one should be baptized who is not intending to come under Jesus' authority by submitting to his church. The affirmation given by a passport goes hand-in-hand with the responsibility and accountability of citizenship. For a new believer, baptism should be the means by which and the moment at which someone joins your church. If you have a membership process consisting of classes and an interview and a congregational vote, the person should go through those steps before being baptized. And the church should understand that membership is being conferred *in* baptism.

Further, churches should not insert a waiting period between baptism and membership. Some might do this out of a desire to emphasize baptism. They decouple baptism from membership in an attempt to draw more attention to baptism. But the biblical way to draw attention to baptism is to make it the gateway into the church and therefore the entry into the Christian life. On the other hand, some might insert a lag between baptism and membership because membership brings serious responsibilities, and maybe a new believer isn't quite ready for those responsibilities. The problem with that is, every Christian is both required and enabled by God to take his or her place in the body. So if you're willing to affirm someone as a Christian, there's no reason to keep him out of the body. That's the only place he will thrive, responsibilities and all. And if you're hesitant about a person's willingness or ability to jump into the life of the body, perhaps that hesitancy should back you up into reconsidering whether you're ready to affirm his profession of faith through baptism.

Under normal circumstances, baptism and church membership should be inseparable. Theologically, baptism confers church membership. So you shouldn't baptize people without bringing them into the church, and you should confer membership on all whom you baptize. A new believer's membership should be conditional upon baptism and should take effect at baptism.

Context

Where should churches baptize people? Does it have to be in a church building, or at least a church service? Not necessarily. Scripture seems to permit baptisms inside and outside normal "church services"—and the only New Testament examples are the latter. But can we say any more than this?

Baptism is a public profession of faith, and the church is the first and most important public to whom that profession is addressed. Further, since baptism is the whole church's act of affirming a believer's profession and welcoming him or her into their number, I would argue that churches should normally baptize people in the context of a whole-church gathering. Whether that gathering is in a church building or down by the river doesn't matter much. The point is that a church's practice of baptism should not obscure but rather highlight the fact that, in baptism, the whole church speaks for God to the individual, and the individual speaks to both God and the whole church. Baptizing in a whole-church gathering broadcasts this; baptizing in a smaller gathering mutes it.

Again thinking of frontier missionary contexts, I'd suggest that a "public" beyond the baptizer is not absolutely necessary to the rite, since the baptizer is himself a public witness to the profession of faith. Yet such "audience of one" baptisms are fitting only when other witnesses are unavailable. Normally, baptism should be celebrated by the whole church since it is an act of the whole church.

Timing

Finally, how quickly should churches baptize new believers? Should new believers be baptized immediately or should there be a waiting period?

Certainly, all the examples of baptism we have in the New Testament happened as soon as someone came to faith. (See, for example, Acts 2:38–41; 10:47–48; 16:14–15, 30–34; 19:1–5). And since baptism is where faith goes public, it should be linked to a person's conversion as closely as possible. So, on the one hand, I don't think churches should insert a waiting period before baptism to either test the fruit of someone's faith or to teach him the basics of Christian faith and practice before baptizing him.

But if baptism should confer church membership, should we be bothered by the fact that the church's membership process slows down the baptism by a few weeks or even months? Isn't this delaying baptism, contrary to the biblical pattern? Not exactly. The church membership process does not amount to a probationary period. Instead, it simply ensures that the baptismal candidate knows what he's getting into and that the church knows the candidate.

At Pentecost, it was pretty clear what you were signing up for: opposition from the Jewish leaders and a whole new life among this persecuted band of the Messiah's followers. Today, things aren't always so clear. There are professing Christians who think that being a Christian has nothing to do with submitting to Jesus' Lordship and nothing to do with the local church. A church needs to ensure that those it baptizes know that living as a Christian has everything to do with submitting to Jesus' Lordship and everything to do with the church. The instruction and assessment involved in a church's membership process simply clarify what's at stake in baptism. And they ensure that those making promises in baptism—both church and believer—know what they're promising and to whom. Requiring baptismal candidates to go through the church's membership process helps ensure that baptism really does draw a line between the church and the world, really does enact a believer's commitment to Christ and his people, really does fulfill Jesus' intent of marking off his people through identifying them with him.

So, to be clear, I don't think churches in the Christianized West, and especially in what's left of the Bible Belt, should hold services in which anyone can come up to the front and be baptized, on the spot, with no commitment to church membership. Such professions of faith are more anonymous than public, since they allow the baptized person to simply go his or her way, disappearing back into the crowd.

If you live in a Muslim country where being baptized means being disowned by your family, the situation is much clearer. But especially for those of us in America, the wisest course is to ensure ahead of time that a believer knows what he or she is signing up for. And churches need to ensure that what those baptized are signing up for is church membership and a life lived under Christ's Lordship.

The Big Deal

In this little book we began with a biblical vision of baptism and wound up in the nuts and bolts. Through it all we've seen something of the who, what, when, where, and especially the why of baptism. If you're a believer in Jesus and your questions about baptism have made you hesitant to be baptized, I hope this book has cleared up those questions and cleared the way for you to obey Jesus by publicly committing yourself to him and his people in baptism. If you're a church leader, I hope you've found some help here for understanding baptism, teaching on baptism, and leading your church in the practice of baptism.

What's the big deal about baptism? Baptism stamps God's people with a sign of the gospel. It calls forth a believer's public commitment to Christ, setting him or her on a lifelong track of open witness to the grace of God in the gospel. It seals a believer's commitment to Christ's people, setting him or her within the fellowship of Christ's body. It speaks a word of affirmation and acceptance from the church to the believer on behalf of Christ. All this is why Jesus commands his disciples to baptize and be baptized.

Baptism pictures and promotes the gospel. And baptism designates and draws a line around the people of the gospel—those who have repented of sin and trusted in Christ. Baptism matters because of the gospel it so vividly signifies.

NOTES

1. This section draws heavily from Jonathan Leeman, *Don't Fire Your Church Members: The Case for Congregationalism* (Nashville, TN: B&H, 2016), chapters 3 and 4.

2. See http://www.9marks.org/church-search.

3. For an exemplary defense of this view, see Sinclair B. Ferguson, "Infant Baptism View," in *Baptism: Three Views,* ed. David F. Wright (Downers Grove, IL: InterVarsity, 2009), 77–111.

4. B. B. Warfield, *Studies in Theology* (New York: Oxford University Press, 1932), 408.

5. At various points in this section I'm drawing on Bruce A. Ware, "Believers' Baptism View," in *Baptism: Three Views*, 19–50.

6. Frank Thielman, *Ephesians*, BECNT (Grand Rapids, MI: Baker, 2010), 397.

7. For the full version of this chapter's argument, see my book *Going Public: Why Baptism Is Required for Church Membership* (Nashville, TN: B&H, 2015). This chapter adapts chapter 8 and portions of chapter 9 of *Going Public*, though it draws on the whole book.

8. John L. Dagg, *Manual of Church Order* (Harrisonburg, VA: Gano Books, 1990), 95.

9. See my article, "You Asked: Should I Get 'Re-Baptized'? (Credobaptist Answer)," at http://thegospelcoalition.org/blogs/tgc/2013/02/06/you-asked-should-i-get-re-baptized-credobaptist-answer.

SCRIPTURE INDEX